BOOK LIFE

A BOOK LOVER'S JOURNAL

COMPILED BY

William McKay

ROCK
POINT

Quarto is the authority on a wide range of topics.

Quarto educates, entertains and enriches the lives of
our readers—enthusiasts and lovers of hands-on living.

www.quartoknows.com

© 2017 Quarto Publishing Group USA Inc.

First published in the United States of America in 2017 by
Rock Point Gift and Stationery, a member of
Quarto Publishing Group USA Inc.
142 West 36th Street, 4th Floor
New York, New York 10018
www.quartoknows.com

10 9 8 7 6 5 4 3 2 1
ISBN 978-1-63106-297-1
Printed in China

MIX
Paper from
responsible sources
FSC® C016973

TABLE OF CONTENTS

66

A book, too,
can be a star,
a living fire to
lighten the darkness,
leading out
into the
expanded universe.

99

—Madeleine L'Engle

Introduction

"A reader lives a thousand lives before he dies. . . . *The man who never reads lives only one.*" George R. R. Martin's words might stand as the motto of millions of men and women for whom books are essential daily companions. Whether fiction or nonfiction, the little paper objects that Stephen King called "uniquely portable magic" inhabit our lives with their stories, but also with their mysteries. Finding out what's next or what's behind the curtain becomes its own reward. As the author's partner in crime, we keep our night-light burning, always leading us to a conclusion that beckons us on to the next book. Thus reading becomes a lifetime journey through space and time, a voyage that renews us even as it reminds us we are not alone.

Franz Kafka described books as the axes, or icebreakers, for the frozen seas within us. What then is a reader's journal? Perhaps if clearly seen and attentively kept, it is an explorer's log to discoveries and ports of call along the way, pointers to finding ourselves amidst blizzards of information.

"

To learn to read
is to light
a fire;
every syllable
that is
spelled out
is a spark.

"

–Victor Hugo

Reading Wish List

So many books, so little time." Frank Zappa was right. Our ever-expanding mental list of what we want to read always makes us second-guess our own choices of what we do read. Wise readers have no compunctions about following the practice of bookseller's son Samuel Johnson, who once responded to a friend's inquiry with a tart, "No, sir, do you read books *through*?"

However you deal with it, your lifetime reading wish list beckons. Do you want to finally immerse yourself in sprawling Russian epics or catch up on Dickens or the thirty-eight Discworld novels you might have missed? Or perhaps you would love to carve out time for the three volumes of Shelby Foote's Civil War histories that have been gathering dust on your shelves ever since you discovered them at the secondhand book sale.

Your personal wish list might be on any topic, genre, period, or author. (Who among us hasn't yearned to read every book by a favorite author?) *What matters is that even though we know we can't read everything we want in our multimillion book world, we keep reaching and reading and gathering in the goodies . . .*

Reading Wish List

❧ Read ☐   Date Completed
_____

Title
_____

Author
_____

Where I heard about it
_____

_____

_____

Why I want to read it
_____

_____

_____

❧ Read ☐   Date Completed
_____

Title
_____

Author
_____

Where I heard about it
_____

_____

_____

Why I want to read it
_____

_____

☙ Read ☐   Date Completed

Title _____

Author _____

Where I heard about it _____

_____

_____

Why I want to read it _____

_____

_____

☙ Read ☐   Date Completed

Title _____

Author _____

Where I heard about it _____

_____

_____

Why I want to read it _____

_____

Reading Wish List

🌿 Read ☐   Date Completed

Title

Author

Where I heard about it

_____

_____

Why I want to read it

_____

_____

🌿 Read ☐   Date Completed

Title

Author

Where I heard about it

_____

_____

Why I want to read it

_____

_____

≉ Read ☐   Date Completed
_____

Title
_____

Author
_____

Where I heard about it
_____

_____

_____

Why I want to read it
_____

_____

_____

≉ Read ☐   Date Completed
_____

Title
_____

Author
_____

Where I heard about it
_____

_____

_____

Why I want to read it
_____

_____

Reading Wish List

❧ Read ☐   Date Completed
_____

Title
_____

Author
_____

Where I heard about it
_____

_____

_____

Why I want to read it
_____

_____

_____

❧ Read ☐   Date Completed
_____

Title
_____

Author
_____

Where I heard about it
_____

_____

_____

Why I want to read it
_____

_____

❧ Read ☐   Date Completed
_____

Title
_____

Author
_____

Where I heard about it
_____

_____

_____

Why I want to read it
_____

_____

_____

❧ Read ☐   Date Completed
_____

Title
_____

Author
_____

Where I heard about it
_____

_____

_____

Why I want to read it
_____

_____

Reading Wish List

❧ Read ☐   Date Completed

Title

Author

Where I heard about it

Why I want to read it

❧ Read ☐   Date Completed

Title

Author

Where I heard about it

Why I want to read it

❧ Read ☐   Date Completed

Title

Author

Where I heard about it

Why I want to read it

❧ Read ☐   Date Completed

Title

Author

Where I heard about it

Why I want to read it

Reading Wish List

※ Read ☐   Date Completed
___

Title
___

Author
___

Where I heard about it
___

___

___

Why I want to read it
___

___

___

※ Read ☐   Date Completed
___

Title
___

Author
___

Where I heard about it
___

___

___

Why I want to read it
___

___

❧ Read ☐   Date Completed
_____

Title
_____

Author
_____

Where I heard about it
_____

_____

_____

Why I want to read it
_____

_____

_____

❧ Read ☐   Date Completed
_____

Title
_____

Author
_____

Where I heard about it
_____

_____

_____

Why I want to read it
_____

_____

Reading Wish List

✻ Read ☐   Date Completed
_____

Title
_____

Author
_____

Where I heard about it
_____

_____

_____

Why I want to read it
_____

_____

_____

✻ Read ☐   Date Completed
_____

Title
_____

Author
_____

Where I heard about it
_____

_____

_____

Why I want to read it
_____

_____

❧ Read ☐   Date Completed _____

Title _____

Author _____

Where I heard about it _____

_____

_____

Why I want to read it _____

_____

_____

❧ Read ☐   Date Completed _____

Title _____

Author _____

Where I heard about it _____

_____

_____

Why I want to read it _____

_____

Reading Wish List

❋ Read ☐   Date Completed
_____

Title
_____

Author
_____

Where I heard about it
_____

_____

_____

Why I want to read it
_____

_____

_____

❋ Read ☐   Date Completed
_____

Title
_____

Author
_____

Where I heard about it
_____

_____

_____

Why I want to read it
_____

_____

❧ Read ☐   Date Completed

Title

Author

Where I heard about it

Why I want to read it

❧ Read ☐   Date Completed

Title

Author

Where I heard about it

Why I want to read it

"

*I cannot remember
the books I've read*
any more
than the meals
I've eaten;
even so,
they have made me.

"

—Ralph Waldo Emerson

My Book Log

According to a 2014 Pew Research Center survey, a typical American reads five books a year. The number of books you read most likely surpasses that number, but even if the lesser tally is accurate, it still amounts to dozens and dozens of books perused over a lifetime. Over time, however, memories of those books, even of their titles, dissolve as we move forward.

In an incandescent passage, Ursula K. Le Guin wrote, "The unread story is not a story; it is little black marks on wood pulp. The reader, reading it, makes it live: a live thing, a story." A book log keeps the stories alive with your own notes, thoughts, and quotes. Attentively kept, it becomes a diary of the mind, a record of the things that keep us going.

My Book Log

Date _____ Overall Grade **A B C D F**

Title _____

Author _____

My thoughts about this book

_____

_____

_____

_____

_____

_____

_____

_____

Memorable ideas or quotes

_____

_____

_____

_____

_____

_____

_____

_____

_____

_____

_____

RATE THIS BOOK

Ease of reading	A B C D F
Memorable characters	A B C D F
Originality	A B C D F
Quality of writing	A B C D F
Read other books by this author?	Y or N
Would you read it again?	Y or N

My Book Log

Date _____ Overall Grade **A B C D F**

Title _____

Author _____

My thoughts about this book

_____

_____

_____

_____

_____

_____

_____

_____

Memorable ideas or quotes

_____

_____

_____

_____

_____

_____

_____

_____

_____

_____

_____

RATE THIS BOOK

Ease of reading	A B C D F
Memorable characters	A B C D F
Originality	A B C D F
Quality of writing	A B C D F
Read other books by this author?	Y or N
Would you read it again?	Y or N

My Book Log

Date _____ Overall Grade **A B C D F**

Title _____

Author _____

My thoughts about this book _____

_____

_____

_____

_____

_____

_____

_____

Memorable ideas or quotes _____

_____

_____

_____

_____

_____

_____

_____

_____

_____

_____

RATE THIS BOOK

Ease of reading		A B C D F
Memorable characters		A B C D F
Originality		A B C D F
Quality of writing		A B C D F
Read other books by this author?		Y or N
Would you read it again?		Y or N

My Book Log

Date _____ Overall Grade **A B C D F**

Title _____

Author _____

My thoughts about this book _____

_____

_____

_____

_____

_____

_____

_____

_____

Memorable ideas or quotes _____

_____

_____

_____

_____

_____

_____

_____

_____

_____

RATE THIS BOOK

Ease of reading	A B C D F	
Memorable characters	A B C D F	
Originality	A B C D F	
Quality of writing	A B C D F	
Read other books by this author?	Y or N	
Would you read it again?	Y or N	

My Book Log

Date _____ Overall Grade **A B C D F**

Title _____

Author _____

My thoughts about this book
_____
_____
_____
_____
_____
_____
_____
_____

Memorable ideas or quotes
_____
_____
_____
_____

_____

_____

_____

_____

_____

_____

_____

RATE THIS BOOK

Ease of reading	A B C D F
Memorable characters	A B C D F
Originality	A B C D F
Quality of writing	A B C D F
Read other books by this author?	Y or N
Would you read it again?	Y or N

My Book Log

Date _____ Overall Grade **A B C D F**

Title _____

Author _____

My thoughts about this book _____

_____

_____

_____

_____

_____

_____

_____

Memorable ideas or quotes _____

_____

_____

_____

RATE THIS BOOK

Ease of reading	A	B	C	D	F
Memorable characters	A	B	C	D	F
Originality	A	B	C	D	F
Quality of writing	A	B	C	D	F
Read other books by this author?	Y	or	N		
Would you read it again?	Y	or	N		

My Book Log

Date _____ Overall Grade   **A**   **B**   **C**   **D**   **F**

Title _____

Author _____

My thoughts about this book
_____

_____

_____

_____

_____

_____

_____

_____

Memorable ideas or quotes
_____

_____

_____

_____

_____

_____

_____

_____

_____

_____

_____

RATE THIS BOOK

Ease of reading	A B C D F
Memorable characters	A B C D F
Originality	A B C D F
Quality of writing	A B C D F
Read other books by this author?	Y or N
Would you read it again?	Y or N

My Book Log

Date _____ Overall Grade **A B C D F**

Title _____

Author _____

My thoughts about this book _____

_____

_____

_____

_____

_____

_____

_____

_____

Memorable ideas or quotes _____

_____

_____

_____

_____

_____

_____

_____

_____

_____

_____

RATE THIS BOOK

Ease of reading	A B C D F
Memorable characters	A B C D F
Originality	A B C D F
Quality of writing	A B C D F
Read other books by this author?	Y or N
Would you read it again?	Y or N

My Book Log

Date _____ Overall Grade **A B C D F**

Title _____

Author _____

My thoughts about this book _____

_____

_____

_____

_____

_____

_____

_____

Memorable ideas or quotes _____

_____

_____

_____

_____

_____

_____

_____

_____

_____

RATE THIS BOOK

Ease of reading	A B C D F
Memorable characters	A B C D F
Originality	A B C D F
Quality of writing	A B C D F
Read other books by this author?	Y or N
Would you read it again?	Y or N

My Book Log

Date _____ Overall Grade **A B C D F**

Title _____

Author _____

My thoughts about this book _____

_____

_____

_____

_____

_____

_____

_____

Memorable ideas or quotes _____

_____

_____

_____

_____

_____

_____

_____

_____

_____

_____

RATE THIS BOOK

Ease of reading	A B C D F
Memorable characters	A B C D F
Originality	A B C D F
Quality of writing	A B C D F
Read other books by this author?	Y or N
Would you read it again?	Y or N

My Book Log

Date _____ Overall Grade **A** **B** **C** **D** **F**

Title _____

Author _____

My thoughts about this book _____

_____

_____

_____

_____

_____

_____

_____

Memorable ideas or quotes _____

_____

_____

_____

RATE THIS BOOK

Ease of reading	A B C D F
Memorable characters	A B C D F
Originality	A B C D F
Quality of writing	A B C D F
Read other books by this author?	Y or N
Would you read it again?	Y or N

My Book Log

Date _____ Overall Grade **A B C D F**

Title _____

Author _____

My thoughts about this book _____

_____

_____

_____

_____

_____

_____

_____

_____

Memorable ideas or quotes _____

_____

_____

_____

_____

_____

_____

_____

_____

_____

_____

_____

RATE THIS BOOK

Ease of reading   A   B   C   D   F

Memorable characters   A   B   C   D   F

Originality   A   B   C   D   F

Quality of writing   A   B   C   D   F

Read other books by this author?   Y   or   N

Would you read it again?   Y   or   N

My Book Log

Date _____ Overall Grade **A B C D F**

Title _____

Author _____

My thoughts about this book _____

_____

_____

_____

_____

_____

_____

_____

Memorable ideas or quotes _____

_____

_____

_____

RATE THIS BOOK

Ease of reading	A B C D F
Memorable characters	A B C D F
Originality	A B C D F
Quality of writing	A B C D F
Read other books by this author?	Y or N
Would you read it again?	Y or N

My Book Log

Date _____ Overall Grade **A B C D F**

Title _____

Author _____

My thoughts about this book
_____

_____

_____

_____

_____

_____

_____

Memorable ideas or quotes
_____

_____

_____

_____

_____

_____

_____

_____

_____

_____

_____

RATE THIS BOOK

Ease of reading   A B C D F

Memorable characters   A B C D F

Originality   A B C D F

Quality of writing   A B C D F

Read other books by this author?   Y   or   N

Would you read it again?   Y   or   N

My Book Log

Date _____ Overall Grade **A B C D F**

Title _____

Author _____

My thoughts about this book _____

_____

_____

_____

_____

_____

_____

_____

Memorable ideas or quotes _____

_____

_____

_____

_____

_____

_____

_____

_____

_____

_____

RATE THIS BOOK

Ease of reading	**A B C D F**
Memorable characters	**A B C D F**
Originality	**A B C D F**
Quality of writing	**A B C D F**
Read other books by this author?	**Y** or **N**
Would you read it again?	**Y** or **N**

My Book Log

Date _____ Overall Grade **A B C D F**

Title _____

Author _____

My thoughts about this book
_____
_____
_____
_____
_____
_____
_____

Memorable ideas or quotes
_____
_____
_____
_____

_____

_____

_____

_____

_____

_____

_____

RATE THIS BOOK

Ease of reading	A	B	C	D	F
Memorable characters	A	B	C	D	F
Originality	A	B	C	D	F
Quality of writing	A	B	C	D	F
Read other books by this author?	Y	or	N		
Would you read it again?	Y	or	N		

My Book Log

Date _____ Overall Grade **A** **B** **C** **D** **F**

Title _____

Author _____

My thoughts about this book
_____
_____
_____
_____
_____
_____
_____
_____

Memorable ideas or quotes
_____
_____
_____
_____

_____

_____

_____

_____

_____

_____

_____

RATE THIS BOOK

Ease of reading	A B C D F
Memorable characters	A B C D F
Originality	A B C D F
Quality of writing	A B C D F
Read other books by this author?	Y or N
Would you read it again?	Y or N

My Book Log

Date _____ Overall Grade **A B C D F**

Title _____

Author _____

My thoughts about this book _____

_____

_____

_____

_____

_____

_____

_____

Memorable ideas or quotes _____

_____

_____

_____

_____

_____

_____

_____

_____

_____

_____

RATE THIS BOOK

Ease of reading	A B C D F
Memorable characters	A B C D F
Originality	A B C D F
Quality of writing	A B C D F
Read other books by this author?	Y or N
Would you read it again?	Y or N

My Book Log

Date _____ Overall Grade **A B C D F**

Title _____

Author _____

My thoughts about this book _____

_____

_____

_____

_____

_____

_____

_____

Memorable ideas or quotes _____

_____

_____

_____

_____

_____

_____

_____

_____

_____

_____

_____

RATE THIS BOOK

Ease of reading	**A**	**B**	**C**	**D**	**F**
Memorable characters	**A**	**B**	**C**	**D**	**F**
Originality	**A**	**B**	**C**	**D**	**F**
Quality of writing	**A**	**B**	**C**	**D**	**F**
Read other books by this author?	**Y**	or	**N**		
Would you read it again?	**Y**	or	**N**		

My Book Log

Date _____ Overall Grade **A B C D F**

Title _____

Author _____

My thoughts about this book

_____

_____

_____

_____

_____

_____

_____

_____

Memorable ideas or quotes

_____

_____

_____

_____

_____

_____

_____

_____

_____

_____

_____

RATE THIS BOOK

Ease of reading	A B C D F
Memorable characters	A B C D F
Originality	A B C D F
Quality of writing	A B C D F
Read other books by this author?	Y or N
Would you read it again?	Y or N

My Book Log

Date _____ Overall Grade **A B C D F**

Title _____

Author _____

My thoughts about this book _____

_____

_____

_____

_____

_____

_____

_____

Memorable ideas or quotes _____

_____

_____

_____

_____

_____

_____

_____

_____

_____

_____

RATE THIS BOOK

Ease of reading	A B C D F	
Memorable characters	A B C D F	
Originality	A B C D F	
Quality of writing	A B C D F	
Read other books by this author?	Y or N	
Would you read it again?	Y or N	

My Book Log

Date _____ Overall Grade **A** **B** **C** **D** **F**

Title _____

Author _____

My thoughts about this book _____

_____

_____

_____

_____

_____

_____

_____

Memorable ideas or quotes _____

_____

_____

_____

_____

RATE THIS BOOK

Ease of reading	A B C D F
Memorable characters	A B C D F
Originality	A B C D F
Quality of writing	A B C D F
Read other books by this author?	Y or N
Would you read it again?	Y or N

My Book Log

Date   Overall Grade   **A B C D F**

Title

Author

My thoughts about this book

Memorable ideas or quotes

_____

_____

_____

_____

_____

_____

_____

RATE THIS BOOK

Ease of reading	A B C D F
Memorable characters	A B C D F
Originality	A B C D F
Quality of writing	A B C D F
Read other books by this author?	Y or N
Would you read it again?	Y or N

My Book Log

Date _____ Overall Grade **A B C D F**

Title _____

Author _____

My thoughts about this book _____

_____

_____

_____

_____

_____

_____

_____

Memorable ideas or quotes _____

_____

_____

_____

_____

_____

_____

_____

_____

_____

_____

RATE THIS BOOK

Ease of reading	A B C D F
Memorable characters	A B C D F
Originality	A B C D F
Quality of writing	A B C D F
Read other books by this author?	Y or N
Would you read it again?	Y or N

My Book Log

Date _____ Overall Grade **A B C D F**

Title _____

Author _____

My thoughts about this book _____

_____

_____

_____

_____

_____

_____

_____

Memorable ideas or quotes _____

_____

_____

_____

_____

_____

_____

_____

_____

_____

_____

RATE THIS BOOK

Ease of reading	A B C D F
Memorable characters	A B C D F
Originality	A B C D F
Quality of writing	A B C D F
Read other books by this author?	Y or N
Would you read it again?	Y or N

My Book Log

Date _____ Overall Grade **A B C D F**

Title _____

Author _____

My thoughts about this book _____

_____

_____

_____

_____

_____

_____

Memorable ideas or quotes _____

_____

_____

_____

_____

_____

_____

_____

_____

_____

_____

RATE THIS BOOK

Ease of reading	A B C D F
Memorable characters	A B C D F
Originality	A B C D F
Quality of writing	A B C D F
Read other books by this author?	Y or N
Would you read it again?	Y or N

My Book Log

Date _____ Overall Grade **A B C D F**

Title _____

Author _____

My thoughts about this book _____

_____

_____

_____

_____

_____

_____

Memorable ideas or quotes _____

_____

_____

_____

_____

_____

_____

_____

_____

_____

_____

RATE THIS BOOK

Ease of reading	A B C D F
Memorable characters	A B C D F
Originality	A B C D F
Quality of writing	A B C D F
Read other books by this author?	Y or N
Would you read it again?	Y or N

My Book Log

Date _____ Overall Grade **A B C D F**

Title _____

Author _____

My thoughts about this book _____

_____

_____

_____

_____

_____

_____

_____

_____

Memorable ideas or quotes _____

_____

_____

_____

_____

_____

_____

_____

_____

_____

_____

_____

RATE THIS BOOK

Ease of reading	A B C D F
Memorable characters	A B C D F
Originality	A B C D F
Quality of writing	A B C D F
Read other books by this author?	Y or N
Would you read it again?	Y or N

My Book Log

Date   Overall Grade   **A B C D F**

Title

Author

My thoughts about this book

_____

_____

_____

_____

_____

_____

_____

Memorable ideas or quotes

_____

_____

_____

_____

_____

_____

_____

_____

_____

_____

_____

RATE THIS BOOK

Ease of reading	A B C D F
Memorable characters	A B C D F
Originality	A B C D F
Quality of writing	A B C D F
Read other books by this author?	Y or N
Would you read it again?	Y or N

My Book Log

Date _____ Overall Grade **A B C D F**

Title _____

Author _____

My thoughts about this book _____

_____

_____

_____

_____

_____

_____

_____

Memorable ideas or quotes _____

_____

_____

_____

_____

_____

_____

_____

_____

_____

RATE THIS BOOK

Ease of reading	A B C D F
Memorable characters	A B C D F
Originality	A B C D F
Quality of writing	A B C D F
Read other books by this author?	Y or N
Would you read it again?	Y or N

My Book Log

Date _____ Overall Grade **A B C D F**

Title _____

Author _____

My thoughts about this book _____

_____

_____

_____

_____

_____

_____

_____

Memorable ideas or quotes _____

_____

_____

_____

Ease of reading	A B C D F
Memorable characters	A B C D F
Originality	A B C D F
Quality of writing	A B C D F
Read other books by this author?	Y or N
Would you read it again?	Y or N

My Book Log

Date _____ Overall Grade **A** **B** **C** **D** **F**

Title _____

Author _____

My thoughts about this book _____

_____

_____

_____

_____

_____

_____

_____

Memorable ideas or quotes _____

_____

_____

_____

_____

_____

_____

_____

_____

_____

_____

RATE THIS BOOK

Ease of reading	**A B C D F**
Memorable characters	**A B C D F**
Originality	**A B C D F**
Quality of writing	**A B C D F**
Read other books by this author?	**Y** or **N**
Would you read it again?	**Y** or **N**

My Book Log

Date _____ Overall Grade **A B C D F**

Title _____

Author _____

My thoughts about this book _____

_____

_____

_____

_____

_____

_____

_____

Memorable ideas or quotes _____

_____

_____

_____

_____

_____

_____

_____

_____

_____

_____

RATE THIS BOOK

Ease of reading	A B C D F
Memorable characters	A B C D F
Originality	A B C D F
Quality of writing	A B C D F
Read other books by this author?	Y or N
Would you read it again?	Y or N

My Book Log

Date _____ Overall Grade **A B C D F**

Title _____

Author _____

My thoughts about this book _____

_____

_____

_____

_____

_____

_____

Memorable ideas or quotes _____

_____

_____

_____

_____

_____

_____

_____

_____

_____

_____

RATE THIS BOOK

Ease of reading	A B C D F
Memorable characters	A B C D F
Originality	A B C D F
Quality of writing	A B C D F
Read other books by this author?	Y or N
Would you read it again?	Y or N

My Book Log

Date _____ Overall Grade **A B C D F**

Title _____

Author _____

My thoughts about this book
_____
_____
_____
_____
_____
_____
_____
_____

Memorable ideas or quotes
_____
_____
_____
_____

_____

_____

_____

_____

_____

_____

_____

RATE THIS BOOK

Ease of reading	A B C D F
Memorable characters	A B C D F
Originality	A B C D F
Quality of writing	A B C D F
Read other books by this author?	Y or N
Would you read it again?	Y or N

My Book Log

Date _____ Overall Grade **A** **B** **C** **D** **F**

Title _____

Author _____

My thoughts about this book

_____

_____

_____

_____

_____

_____

_____

Memorable ideas or quotes _____

_____

_____

_____

_____

_____

_____

_____

_____

_____

_____

RATE THIS BOOK

Ease of reading	**A** **B** **C** **D** **F**
Memorable characters	**A** **B** **C** **D** **F**
Originality	**A** **B** **C** **D** **F**
Quality of writing	**A** **B** **C** **D** **F**
Read other books by this author?	**Y** or **N**
Would you read it again?	**Y** or **N**

My Book Log

Date _____   Overall Grade **A B C D F**

Title _____

Author _____

My thoughts about this book _____

_____

_____

_____

_____

_____

_____

_____

Memorable ideas or quotes _____

_____

_____

_____

_____

_____

_____

_____

_____

_____

_____

RATE THIS BOOK

Ease of reading	A B C D F
Memorable characters	A B C D F
Originality	A B C D F
Quality of writing	A B C D F
Read other books by this author?	Y or N
Would you read it again?	Y or N

My Book Log

Date _____   Overall Grade **A B C D F**

Title _____

Author _____

My thoughts about this book

_____

_____

_____

_____

_____

_____

_____

Memorable ideas or quotes

_____

_____

_____

_____

_____

_____

_____

_____

_____

_____

_____

RATE THIS BOOK

Ease of reading	A	B	C	D	F
Memorable characters	A	B	C	D	F
Originality	A	B	C	D	F
Quality of writing	A	B	C	D	F
Read other books by this author?	Y	or	N		
Would you read it again?	Y	or	N		

My Book Log

Date _____   Overall Grade   **A   B   C   D   F**

Title _____

Author _____

My thoughts about this book
_____

_____

_____

_____

_____

_____

_____

_____

Memorable ideas or quotes
_____

_____

_____

_____

_____

_____

_____

_____

_____

_____

_____

RATE THIS BOOK

Ease of reading	A B C D F
Memorable characters	A B C D F
Originality	A B C D F
Quality of writing	A B C D F
Read other books by this author?	Y or N
Would you read it again?	Y or N

My Book Log

Date _____ Overall Grade **A B C D F**

Title _____

Author _____

My thoughts about this book _____

_____

_____

_____

_____

_____

_____

_____

Memorable ideas or quotes _____

_____

_____

_____

_____

_____

_____

_____

_____

_____

_____

RATE THIS BOOK

Ease of reading	A B C D F
Memorable characters	A B C D F
Originality	A B C D F
Quality of writing	A B C D F
Read other books by this author?	Y or N
Would you read it again?	Y or N

My Book Log

Date _____ Overall Grade **A B C D F**

Title _____

Author _____

My thoughts about this book

_____

_____

_____

_____

_____

_____

_____

_____

Memorable ideas or quotes

_____

_____

_____

_____

_____

_____

_____

_____

_____

_____

_____

RATE THIS BOOK

Ease of reading	A B C D F
Memorable characters	A B C D F
Originality	A B C D F
Quality of writing	A B C D F
Read other books by this author?	Y or N
Would you read it again?	Y or N

My Book Log

Date _____ Overall Grade **A** **B** **C** **D** **F**

Title _____

Author _____

My thoughts about this book

_____

_____

_____

_____

_____

_____

_____

_____

Memorable ideas or quotes

_____

_____

_____

_____

_____

_____

_____

_____

_____

_____

_____

RATE THIS BOOK

Ease of reading	A	B	C	D	F
Memorable characters	A	B	C	D	F
Originality	A	B	C	D	F
Quality of writing	A	B	C	D	F
Read other books by this author?	Y	or	N		
Would you read it again?	Y	or	N		

My Book Log

Date _____ Overall Grade **A** **B** **C** **D** **F**

Title _____

Author _____

My thoughts about this book
_____
_____
_____
_____
_____
_____
_____
_____

Memorable ideas or quotes
_____
_____
_____
_____

_____

_____

_____

_____

_____

_____

_____

RATE THIS BOOK

Ease of reading	A B C D F
Memorable characters	A B C D F
Originality	A B C D F
Quality of writing	A B C D F
Read other books by this author?	Y or N
Would you read it again?	Y or N

My Book Log

Date _____ Overall Grade **A B C D F**

Title _____

Author _____

My thoughts about this book _____

_____

_____

_____

_____

_____

_____

_____

Memorable ideas or quotes _____

_____

_____

_____

Ease of reading	A B C D F
Memorable characters	A B C D F
Originality	A B C D F
Quality of writing	A B C D F
Read other books by this author?	Y or N
Would you read it again?	Y or N

My Book Log

Date _____ Overall Grade **A B C D F**

Title _____

Author _____

My thoughts about this book
_____

_____

_____

_____

_____

_____

_____

_____

Memorable ideas or quotes
_____

_____

_____

_____

_____

_____

_____

_____

_____

_____

_____

RATE THIS BOOK

Ease of reading	A B C D F
Memorable characters	A B C D F
Originality	A B C D F
Quality of writing	A B C D F
Read other books by this author?	Y or N
Would you read it again?	Y or N

My Book Log

Date _____ Overall Grade **A B C D F**

Title _____

Author _____

My thoughts about this book
_____
_____
_____
_____
_____
_____
_____
_____

Memorable ideas or quotes
_____
_____
_____
_____

_____

_____

_____

_____

_____

_____

_____

_____

RATE THIS BOOK

Ease of reading	A B C D F
Memorable characters	A B C D F
Originality	A B C D F
Quality of writing	A B C D F
Read other books by this author?	Y or N
Would you read it again?	Y or N

My Book Log

Date _____ Overall Grade **A B C D F**

Title _____

Author _____

My thoughts about this book
_____

_____

_____

_____

_____

_____

_____

_____

Memorable ideas or quotes
_____

_____

_____

_____

_____

_____

_____

_____

_____

_____

_____

RATE THIS BOOK

Ease of reading	A B C D F
Memorable characters	A B C D F
Originality	A B C D F
Quality of writing	A B C D F
Read other books by this author?	Y or N
Would you read it again?	Y or N

My Book Log

Date _____ Overall Grade **A B C D F**

Title _____

Author _____

My thoughts about this book _____

_____

_____

_____

_____

_____

_____

_____

Memorable ideas or quotes _____

_____

_____

_____

_____

_____

_____

_____

_____

_____

_____

RATE THIS BOOK

Ease of reading	A B C D F
Memorable characters	A B C D F
Originality	A B C D F
Quality of writing	A B C D F
Read other books by this author?	Y or N
Would you read it again?	Y or N

My Book Log

Date _____ Overall Grade **A B C D F**

Title _____

Author _____

My thoughts about this book

_____

_____

_____

_____

_____

_____

_____

Memorable ideas or quotes

_____

_____

_____

_____

_____

_____

_____

_____

_____

_____

_____

RATE THIS BOOK

Ease of reading	A B C D F
Memorable characters	A B C D F
Originality	A B C D F
Quality of writing	A B C D F
Read other books by this author?	Y or N
Would you read it again?	Y or N

My Book Log

Date _____ Overall Grade **A B C D F**

Title _____

Author _____

My thoughts about this book
_____

_____

_____

_____

_____

_____

_____

_____

Memorable ideas or quotes
_____

_____

_____

_____

_____

_____

_____

_____

_____

_____

_____

RATE THIS BOOK

Ease of reading	A	B	C	D	F
Memorable characters	A	B	C	D	F
Originality	A	B	C	D	F
Quality of writing	A	B	C	D	F
Read other books by this author?	Y	or	N		
Would you read it again?	Y	or	N		

My Book Log

Date _____   Overall Grade **A B C D F**

Title _____

Author _____

My thoughts about this book _____

_____

_____

_____

_____

_____

_____

_____

Memorable ideas or quotes _____

_____

_____

_____

_____

_____

_____

_____

_____

_____

_____

RATE THIS BOOK

Ease of reading	**A B C D F**
Memorable characters	**A B C D F**
Originality	**A B C D F**
Quality of writing	**A B C D F**
Read other books by this author?	**Y** or **N**
Would you read it again?	**Y** or **N**

My Book Log

Date _____   Overall Grade **A B C D F**

Title _____

Author _____

My thoughts about this book _____

_____

_____

_____

_____

_____

_____

_____

Memorable ideas or quotes _____

_____

_____

_____

_____

_____

_____

_____

_____

_____

_____

RATE THIS BOOK

Ease of reading	**A B C D F**
Memorable characters	**A B C D F**
Originality	**A B C D F**
Quality of writing	**A B C D F**
Read other books by this author?	**Y** or **N**
Would you read it again?	**Y** or **N**

My Book Log

Date _____ Overall Grade **A B C D F**

Title _____

Author _____

My thoughts about this book
_____
_____
_____
_____
_____
_____
_____
_____

Memorable ideas or quotes
_____
_____
_____
_____

_____

_____

_____

_____

_____

_____

_____

RATE THIS BOOK

Ease of reading	A B C D F
Memorable characters	A B C D F
Originality	A B C D F
Quality of writing	A B C D F
Read other books by this author?	Y or N
Would you read it again?	Y or N

My Book Log

Date   Overall Grade   **A   B   C   D   F**

Title

Author

My thoughts about this book

_____

_____

_____

_____

_____

_____

_____

Memorable ideas or quotes

_____

_____

_____

_____

_____

_____

_____

_____

_____

_____

_____

RATE THIS BOOK

Ease of reading	A B C D F
Memorable characters	A B C D F
Originality	A B C D F
Quality of writing	A B C D F
Read other books by this author?	Y or N
Would you read it again?	Y or N

My Book Log

Date _____   Overall Grade   **A**   **B**   **C**   **D**   **F**

Title _____

Author _____

My thoughts about this book _____

_____

_____

_____

_____

_____

_____

_____

Memorable ideas or quotes _____

_____

_____

_____

_____

_____

_____

_____

_____

_____

_____

RATE THIS BOOK

Ease of reading	A B C D F
Memorable characters	A B C D F
Originality	A B C D F
Quality of writing	A B C D F
Read other books by this author?	Y or N
Would you read it again?	Y or N

My Book Log

Date _____ Overall Grade **A B C D F**

Title _____

Author _____

My thoughts about this book _____

_____

_____

_____

_____

_____

_____

_____

Memorable ideas or quotes _____

_____

_____

_____

_____

_____

_____

_____

_____

_____

_____

RATE THIS BOOK

Ease of reading	A	B	C	D	F
Memorable characters	A	B	C	D	F
Originality	A	B	C	D	F
Quality of writing	A	B	C	D	F
Read other books by this author?	Y	or	N		
Would you read it again?	Y	or	N		

My Book Log

Date _____ Overall Grade **A B C D F**

Title _____

Author _____

My thoughts about this book _____

_____

_____

_____

_____

_____

_____

_____

Memorable ideas or quotes _____

_____

_____

_____

_____

_____

_____

_____

_____

_____

_____

RATE THIS BOOK

Ease of reading	A B C D F
Memorable characters	A B C D F
Originality	A B C D F
Quality of writing	A B C D F
Read other books by this author?	Y or N
Would you read it again?	Y or N

My Book Log

Date _____ Overall Grade **A B C D F**

Title _____

Author _____

My thoughts about this book
_____
_____
_____
_____
_____
_____
_____
_____

Memorable ideas or quotes
_____
_____
_____
_____

Ease of reading	A B C D F
Memorable characters	A B C D F
Originality	A B C D F
Quality of writing	A B C D F
Read other books by this author?	Y or N
Would you read it again?	Y or N

My Book Log

Date _____ Overall Grade **A B C D F**

Title _____

Author _____

My thoughts about this book
_____
_____
_____
_____
_____
_____
_____
_____

Memorable ideas or quotes
_____
_____
_____
_____

_____

_____

_____

_____

_____

_____

_____

RATE THIS BOOK

Ease of reading	A B C D F
Memorable characters	A B C D F
Originality	A B C D F
Quality of writing	A B C D F
Read other books by this author?	Y or N
Would you read it again?	Y or N

"

Man reading
should be
man intensely alive.
The book should be
a ball of light
in one's hand.

"

—Ezra Pound

Memorable Quotes

Three funny men on books, bookstores, and reading.

Whether we think of them as verbal potted plants or short sentences drawn from long experience, quotations resonate in all of us. Gradually, these memorable snippets become our histories, reminding us that Ralph Waldo Emerson once said that we are all quotations from all our ancestors. Thus, when we jot down a sentence or two or three from a book, we are transplanting it into own experience.

"I find television very educating. Every time somebody turns on the set, I go into the other room and read a book." —Groucho Marx

"Outside of a dog, a book is man's best friend. Inside of a dog it's too dark to read." —Groucho Marx

"From the moment I picked your book up until I laid it down, I convulsed with laughter. Someday I intend reading it." —Groucho Marx

"I took a speed-reading course and read War and Peace in twenty minutes. It involves Russia." —Woody Allen

"I went to a bookstore and asked the saleswoman, 'Where's the self-help section?' She said if she told me, it would defeat the purpose." —George Carlin

"Don't just teach your children to read. Teach them to question what they read. Teach them to question everything." —George Carlin

"

_____

_____

_____

_____

_____

_____

Author: _____

Title: _____

_____

_____

_____

_____

Author: _____

Title: _____

_____

_____

_____

_____

_____

Author: _____

Title: _____

_____

_____

_____

_____

Author: _____

Title: _____

99

"

Author:

Title:

Author:

Title:

_____

_____

_____

_____

_____

_____

Author: _____

Title: _____

_____

_____

_____

_____

_____

Author: _____

Title: _____

99

66

Show me a family
of readers,
and I will show you
the people
who move the world.

99

—Napoleon Bonaparte

My Favorite Books and Authors

According to a recent compilation, the world's five most popular fiction authors are, in order, William Shakespeare, Agatha Christie, Barbara Cartland, Danielle Steel, and Harold Robbins. In our informal research, however, we quickly discovered that whether you are talking about authors or individual books, popular does not equal favorite. In fact, it didn't take us long to encounter a daunting list of favorite writers and an even more staggering roster of their best books. From Ansel Adams to Émile Zola, these primetime authors just kept coming. As for titles, votes were registered for works by everyone from Herodotus to Gillian Flynn.

Even eccentric books attract enthusiasts. Take, for example, Laurence Sterne's *The Life and Opinions of Tristram Shandy, Gentleman*. Dismissed by some as a digressive, bawdy mess, this lengthy eighteenth-century novel has been embraced by writers and philosophers, including James Joyce, Karl Marx, Salman Rushdie, Carlos Fuentes, and Don DeLillo.

There's no accounting for taste; that's what makes it so interesting. Your choices of favorite authors and books will likely surprise others, and they might even surprise you.

My Favorite Books and Authors

In the section below, jot down your best-regarded or even your most whimsical choices for writers and works.

Date
_____

Title
_____

Author
_____

Why I love this book
_____

_____

_____

_____

Date
_____

Title
_____

Author
_____

Why I love this book
_____

_____

_____

Date
_____

Title
_____

Author
_____

Why I love this book
_____

_____

_____

_____

Date
_____

Title
_____

Author
_____

Why I love this book
_____

_____

_____

My Favorite Books and Authors

In the section below, jot down your best-regarded or even your most whimsical choices for writers and works.

Date _____

Title _____

Author _____

Why I love this book _____

_____

_____

_____

Date _____

Title _____

Author _____

Why I love this book _____

_____

_____

Date
_____

Title
_____

Author
_____

Why I love this book
_____

_____

_____

_____

Date
_____

Title
_____

Author
_____

Why I love this book
_____

_____

_____

My Favorite Books
and Authors

In the section below, jot down your best-regarded or
even your most whimsical choices for writers and works.

Date _____

Title _____

Author _____

Why I love this book _____

_____

_____

_____

Date _____

Title _____

Author _____

Why I love this book _____

_____

_____

Date
_____

Title
_____

Author
_____

Why I love this book
_____

_____

_____

_____

Date
_____

Title
_____

Author
_____

Why I love this book
_____

_____

_____

Books That
Changed My Life

Ask a dozen people what books changed their lives (we did), and you will likely receive at least that many different answers. For some people, it could be a children's book or a high school chemistry text; for others, a diet guide that worked, a translation of *Dante's Divine Comedy*, or Mitch Albom's *Tuesdays with Morrie*. One person credited *The Rough Guide to Morocco* with helping him overcome his fear of travel, even as another insisted quite swkeriously that Dr. Seuss' *Oh, The Places You'll Go!* prepared her for her future—"even if it was then just in grade school."

One inveterate reader told us that he became a writer partly because of, all things, James Boswell's *Life of Samuel Johnson*. Robert Pirsig's philosophical novel *Zen and the Art of Motorcycle Maintenance* and Jack Kerouac's classic On the Road are documented to have convinced more than a few college students to refocus their lives.

Authors sometimes find their own life-changing reading in unexpected sources. Mary Higgins Clark is a perennial bestselling mystery writer, but she told an interviewer that it was a reading of Pearl Buck's *The Good Earth*, when she was nine, that convinced her to be a writer. For Alice McDermott, the inspiration came from the maudlin manuscripts that she had to read while working as an editor for a vanity publisher.

What books (note the plural) have set you on a refreshing life path or gifted you with a newfound tranquility? your own notes, thoughts, and quotes. Attentively kept, it becomes a diary of the mind, a record of the things that keep us going.

Books That Changed My Life

Title
_____

Author
_____

Why this book is important to me and how it changed me
_____

_____

_____

_____

_____

Title
_____

Author
_____

Why this book is important to me and how it changed me
_____

_____

_____

_____

Title
_____

Author
_____

Why this book is important to me and how it changed me
_____

_____

_____

_____

_____

Title
_____

Author
_____

Why this book is important to me and how it changed me
_____

_____

_____

_____

_____

Books That Changed
My Life

Title
_____

Author
_____

Why this book is important to me and how it changed me

_____

_____

_____

_____

Title
_____

Author
_____

Why this book is important to me and how it changed me

_____

_____

_____

_____

Title
_____

Author
_____

Why this book is important to me and how it changed me
_____

_____

_____

_____

_____

Title
_____

Author
_____

Why this book is important to me and how it changed me
_____

_____

_____

_____

_____

"

*The reading of
all good books*
is like
a conversation
with the most eminent
people of
past centuries...

"

—René Descartes

Literary Pilgrimages

Visiting the former home of a beloved author can give even the most ardent devotee a deeper sense of who the writer was and how he or she lived. In compiling this gathering of literary landmarks, we metaphorically walked the extra mile to seek destinations that offered more than just a plaque or an apology that the original building had been replaced by a rug store or pie shop. Each of our selections offers not only the immediate context of place, but also an enhanced sense of the author who lived there.

One additional tip:

Each of these landmarks is multifaceted. Most of them have guided tours, many feature additional events, several have gift stores, and all of them have informative websites with directions.

JACK LONDON STATE HISTORIC PARK
2400 London Ranch Road, Glen Ellen, California 95442.
(707) 938-5216

NATIONAL STEINBECK CENTER
1 Main Street, Salinas, California 93901.
(831) 775-4721

THE ERNEST HEMINGWAY HOME & MUSEUM
907 Whitehead Street, Key West, Florida 33040.
(305) 294-1136.

MARGARET MITCHELL HOUSE
990 Peachtree Street NE,
Atlanta, Georgia 30309. (404) 249-7015

ERNEST HEMINGWAY BIRTHPLACE AND MUSEUM
200 North Oak Park Avenue, Oak Park, Illinois 60303.
(708) 445-3071 and (708) 524-5383

THE KURT VONNEGUT MEMORIAL LIBRARY
The Emelie Building, 340 North Senate Avenue,
Indianapolis, Indiana 46204. (317) 652-1954

THE EMILY DICKINSON MUSEUM
280 Main Street, Amherst, Massachusetts 01002.
(413) 542-8161

THE WAYSIDE, HOME OF THE HAWTHORNES AND THE ALCOTTS
Minuteman National Historical Park,
455 Lexington Road, Concord, Massachusetts 01742.
(978) 318-7825

THE MOUNT, EDITH WHARTON'S HOME
2 Plunkett Street, Lenox, Massachusetts 02140.
(413) 551-5111

HERMAN MELVILLE'S ARROWHEAD
780 Holmes Road, Pittsfield, Massachusetts 01201. (413) 442-1793

THE MARK TWAIN BOYHOOD HOME & MUSEUM
North Main Street, Hannibal, Missouri 63401. (573) 221-9010

THE LAURA INGALLS WILDER HISTORIC HOME & MUSEUM
3068 Highway A, Mansfield, Missouri 65704. (877) 924-7126

WILLA CATHER BIRTHPLACE
413 North Webster, Red Cloud, Nebraska 68970. (866) 731-7304

THE WALT WHITMAN BIRTHPLACE HISTORIC SITE
246 Old Whitman Road, Huntington Station, New York 11476.
(631) 427-5240

CHARLES DICKENS HOME AND MUSEUM
48 Doughty Street, London WC1N 2LX, United Kingdom.
+44 20 7405 2127

THE SHERLOCK HOLMES MUSEUM
221b Baker Street, London NW1 6XE, United Kingdom.
+44 207 224 3688

THE SHAKESPEARE BIRTHPLACE TRUST
The Shakespeare Centre, Henley Street,
Stratford Upon Avon, Warwickshire CV37 6QW.
+44 1789 20401

" *I have gone to them [bookshops]*
for years, always finding the
one book I wanted—
and then three more
I hadn't known I wanted. "

—Mary Ann Shaffer

A Selection of Bookstores Worth Visiting

"A book worth reading is worth buying."
—John Ruskin

"Where is human nature so weak as in a bookstore?"
—Henry Ward Beecher

An anonymous sage once said that it's not surprising that many romantic relationships begin in bookstores because so many other meaningful connections are formed there. Many of us can still remember the shop where we first picked up a copy of The Joy of Cooking or thumbed through our first novel by David Baldacci, J. K. Rowling, or Sue Grafton. Those first bookstore encounters were the beginnings of long, important relationships that have outlasted many marriages.

This gathering of notable bookstores is eclectic, personal, sometimes whimsical, and definitely not final or exclusionary. For each state and the District of Columbia, two bookstores were selected, to which a smattering of overseas bookshops were added. The bookstores were chosen because their selection and local staff help generate interest among area booklovers. These independents and chain stores share a sense of purpose in bolstering a community of readers. Mercifully, they are not alone: this list could be doubled and redoubled and redoubled again. Bookstores nurture us in ways that nothing else does.

Jim Reed Books
2021 3rd Avenue N., Birmingham, Alabama 35203. (205) 326-4460

Bienville Books
109 Dauphin Street, Mobile, Alabama 36602. (251) 438-2904

Title Wave Books
1360 W. Northern Lights Boulevard, Anchorage, Alaska 99503.
(904) 278-9283

Fairbanks Barnes & Noble
421 Mehar Avenue, Fairbanks, Alaska 99701. (907) 452-6400

Metro Barnes & Noble
Metro Center, 10235 North Metro Parkway East, Phoenix, Arizona
85051. (602) 678-0088

Changing Hands Bookstore
6428 South McClintock Drive, Tempe, Arizona 85283.
(480) 730-0205

Dickson Street Bookshop
325 West Dickson Street, Fayetteville, Arkansas 72701.
(479) 442-8182

WordsWorth Books & Co.
5920 R Street, Little Rock, Arkansas 72207. (501) 663-9198

The Grove at Farmers Market Barnes & Noble
189 The Grove Drive, Suite K30, Los Angeles, California 90036.
(323) 525-0270

Vroman's Bookstore
695 E. Colorado Blvd., Pasadena, California 91101. (626) 449-5320

Boulder Book Store
1107 Pearl Street, Boulder, Colorado 80302. (303) 447-2074

The Bookies
4315 East Mississippi Avenue, Denver, Colorado 80246. (303) 759-1117

Atticus
1082 Chapel Street, New Haven, Connecticut 06510. (203) 776-4040

The Book Barn
41 West Main Street, Niantic, Connecticut 06357. (860) 739-5715

Captain Blue Hen Comics & Entertainment
80 East Main Street, Suite 101, Newark, Delaware 19711. (302) 737-3434

Christiana Mall Barnes & Noble
340 Christiana Mall, Newark, Delaware 19702. (302) 369-7050

The Bookstore in the Grove
3390 Mary Street, Coconut Grove, Florida 33133. (305) 443-2855

Colonial Drive Barnes & Noble
2418 East Colonial Drive, Orlando, Florida 32803. (407) 894-6024

Bound to Read Books
481 Flat Shoals Avenue, Atlanta, Georgia 30316. (404) 522-0877

Eagle Eye Book Shop
2076 North Decatur Road, Decatur, Georgia 30033. (404) 486-0307

Ala Moana Barnes & Noble
1450 Ala Moana Boulevard, Honolulu, Hawaii 96814. (808) 949-7307

Boise Barnes & Noble
1301 North Milwaukee Street, Boise, Idaho 83704. (208) 375-4454

Chapter One Bookstore
340 East Second Street, Ketchum, Idaho 83340. (208) 726-5425

Myopic Books
1564 North Milwaukee Avenue, Chicago, Illinois 60622.
(773) 862-4882

Unabridged Books
3251 North Broadway, Chicago, Illinois 60657. (773) 883-9119

Half Price Bookstore
4709 East 82nd Street, Indianapolis, Indiana 46250. (317) 577-0410

Indie Reads Books
911 Massachusetts Avenue, Indianapolis, Indiana 46202.
(317) 384-1496

Half Price Books
1400 Twixt Town Road NE, Cedar Rapids, Iowa 52302.
(319) 377-4982

Prairie Lights Bookstore
15 South Dubuque Street, Iowa City, Iowa 52240. (319) 337-2681

Rainy Day Books
2706 West 53rd Street, Fairway, Kansas 66205. (913) 384-3126

Watermark Books & Café
4701 East Douglas, Wichita, Kansas 67218. (316) 682-1181

Joseph-Beth Booksellers
61 Lexington Green Center, Suite B1, Lexington, Kentucky 40503.
(859) 273-2911

Carmichael's Bookstore
1295 Bardstown Road, Louisville, Kentucky 40204. (502) 456-6950

Faulkner House Books
624 Pirates Alley, New Orleans, Louisiana 70116. (504) 524-2940

Shreveport Barnes & Noble
Bayou Walk, 6646 Youree Drive, Shreveport, Louisiana 71105.
(318) 798-6066

Marketplace Drive Barnes & Noble
9 Marketplace Drive, Augusta, Maine 04330. (207) 621-0038

Gulf of Maine Books
34 Maine Street, Brunswick, Maine 04011. (207) 729-5083

The Ivy
6080 Falls Road, Baltimore, Maryland 21209. (410) 377-2966

Kelmscott Bookshop
34 W. 25th Street, Baltimore, Maryland 21218. (410) 235-6810

The Coop
1400 Massachusetts Avenue, Cambridge, Massachusetts 02139.
(617) 499-2000

Baker Books
2 McCabe Street, Dartmouth, Massachusetts 02747. (508) 997-6700

Ann Arbor Barnes & Noble
Huron Village, 3235 Washtenaw Avenue, Ann Arbor, Michigan
48104. (734) 973-0846

John K. King Used & Rare Books
901 West Lafayette Boulevard, Detroit, Michigan 48226.
(313) 961-0622.

Once Upon a Crime
604 West Street, Minneapolis, Minnesota 55405. (612) 870-3785

Roseville II Barnes & Noble
HarMar Mall, 2100 North Snelling Avenue, Roseville,
Minnesota 55113. (651) 639-9256

Square Books
160 Courthouse Square, Oxford, Mississippi 38655. (662) 236-2262

Lorelei Books
1103 Washington Street, Vicksburg, Mississippi 39183. (601) 634-8624

Kansas City Barnes & Noble
400 West 47th Street, Kansas City, Missouri 64112. (816) 753-1313

Subterranean Books
6275 Delmar Boulevard, St. Louis, Missouri 63130. (314) 862-6100

Country Bookshelf
28 West Main, Bozeman, Montana 59715. (406) 587-0166

Bookstore at the University of Montana
Mountain Campus, University Center, 5 Campus Drive,
Missoula, Montana 59801. (406) 243-1234

Haymarket Creamery Building
701 P Street, Suite 102, Lincoln, Nebraska 68508. (402) 477-7770

Jackson Street Booksellers
1119 Jackson Street, Omaha, Nebraska 68102. (402) 341-2664

Northwest Barnes & Noble
Rainbow Promenade, 2191 North Rainbow Boulevard, Las Vegas,
Nevada 89108. (702) 631-1775

Sundance Books and Music
121 California Avenue, Reno, Nevada 89509. (775) 786-1188

Gibson's Bookstore
45 South Maine Street, Concord, New Hampshire 03301.
(603) 224-0562

The Toadstool Bookshop
12 Depot Square, Peterborough, New Hampshire 03458.
(603) 924-3543

Paramus Barnes & Noble
765 Route 17 South, Paramus, New Jersey 07652. (201) 445-4589

The Town Bookstore
270 East Broad Street, Westfield, New Jersey 07090.
(908) 233-3535

BookWorks
4022 Rio Grande Blvd NW, Albuquerque, New Mexico 87107.
(505) 344-8139

Page 1 Bookstore
5850 Eubank Blvd NE, Unit #B41, Albuquerque, New Mexico 87111.
(505) 294-2026

The Strand Bookstore
828 Broadway, New York, New York 10003. (212) 473-1452

Union Square Barnes & Noble
33 East 17th Street, New York, New York 10003. (212) 253-0810

Malaprops Bookstore & Café
55 Haywood Street, Asheville, North Carolina 28801.
(828) 254-6734

Morrison Place Barnes & Noble
4020 Sharon Road, Charlotte, North Carolina 28211. (704) 364-0626

Fargo Barnes & Noble
1201 42 Street SW, Fargo, North Dakota 58103. (701) 281-1002

Main Street Books
106 Main Street South, Minot, North Dakota 58701. (701) 839-4050

Fireside Book Shop
29 North Franklin Street, Chagrin Falls, Ohio 44022.
(440) 247-4050

The Book Loft of German Village
631 South Third Street, Columbus, Ohio 43206. (614) 464-1774

Full Circle Bookstore
50 Penn Place, 1900 NW Expressway, Oklahoma City,
Oklahoma 73118. (405) 842-2900

May Avenue Barnes & Noble
6100 North May Avenue, Oklahoma City, Oklahoma 73112.
(405) 843-9300

Eugene Barnes & Noble
163 Valley River Drive, Eugene, Oregon 97401. (541) 687-0356

Powell's City of Books
1005 West Burnside Street, Portland, Oregon 97209. (503) 228-4651

Rittenhouse Square Barnes & Noble
1805 Walnut Street, Philadelphia, Pennsylvania 19103. (215) 665-0716

The Spiral Bookcase
112 Cotton Street, Philadelphia, Pennsylvania 19127. (215) 482-0704

The Studio at Barrington Books
184 Country Road, Barrington, Rhode Island 02806. (401) 245-7925

Cellar Stories Book Store
11 Mathewson Street, Providence, Rhode Island 02903.
(401) 521-2665

Beaufort Bookstore
2127 Boundary Street, Beaufort, South Carolina 29902.
(843) 525-1066

Hub City Bookstore
186 West Main Street, Spartanburg, South Carolina 29306.
(864) 577-9349

Black Hills Books and Treasures
112 South Chicago Street, Hot Springs, South Dakota 57747.
(605) 745-5545

Zandbroz Variety
209 South Phillips Avenue, Sioux City, South Dakota 57104.
(605) 331-5137

Book Stop Plus
2810 Bartlett Road, Suite 8, Memphis, Tennessee 38134.
(901) 382-222

Germantown Parkway Barnes & Noble
2774 North Germantown Parkway, Memphis, Tennessee 38133.
(901) 386-2468

Lincoln Park Barnes & Noble
7700 West Northwest Highway, Suite 300, Dallas, Texas 75225.
(214) 739-1124

Brazos Bookstore
2421 Bissonnet Street, Houston, Texas 77005. (713) 523-0701

Gateway Barnes & Noble
6 North Rio Grande Street, Salt Lake City, Utah 84101.
(801) 456-0100

Weller Book Works
607 Trolley Square, Salt Lake City, Utah 84102. (801) 328-2586

Northshire Bookstore
4869 Main Street, Manchester Center, Vermont 05255.
(602) 362-2200

Boxcar & Caboose
394 Railroad Street, Suite 2, St. Johnsbury, Vermont 05819.
(802) 748-3551

McKay Used Books
8345 Sudley Road, Manassas, Virginia 20109. (703) 361-9042

Prince Books
109 East Main Street, Norfolk, Virginia 23510. (757) 622-9223

Elliott Bay Bookstore
1521 Tenth Avenue, Seattle, Washington 98122. (206) 624-6600

Magus Used Books
408 NE 42nd Street, Seattle, Washington 98105. (206) 633-1800

Capitol Hill Books
657 C Street SE, Washington, D.C. 20003. (202) 544-1621

Downtown D.C. Barnes & Noble
555 12th Street NW, Washington, D.C. 20004. (202) 347-0176

Mainline Bookstore
301 Davis Avenue, Elkins, West Virginia 26241. (304) 636-6770

Words & Music Bookshop
4 Hyde Park Drive, Wheeling, West Virginia 26003. (304) 232-6539

Greenfield Place
5032 South 74th Street, Greenfield, Wisconsin 53220.
(414) 281-0000

A Room of One's Own
315 West Gorham Street, Madison, Wisconsin 53703. (608) 257-7888

Valley Bookstore
125 North Cache Drive, Jackson, Wyoming 83001. (307) 733-4533

Mad Dog and the Pilgrim Booksellers
4176 Highway 789, Sweetwater Station, Wyoming 82520.
(307) 544-2203

...And half a dozen other world-class English-language bookstores in other parts of the world:

Munro's Books
108 Government Street, Victoria, British Columbia, Canada V8W 1Y2. (250) 382-2464

Shakespeare and Company
37 rue de la Bûcherie, 75005 Paris, France. +33 (0) 1-43-25-40-93

Charlie Byrne's Bookshop
The Cornstore, Middle Street, Galway, Ireland. +353 (0) 91561766

Daunt Books Marylebone
83 Marylebone High Street, London W1U 4QW, United Kingdom. +44 20 7224 2295

Foyle's at Charing Cross
113–119 Charing Cross Road, London WC2H 0EB, United Kingdom. +44 20 7437 5660

Daunt Books
83 Marylebone High Street, London W1U 4QW, United Kingdom +44 207 224 2295

Waterstone's London- Piccadilly
203/206 Piccadilly, London, W1J 9HD, United Kingdom +44 207 851 2400

Tate Modern Shop
Bankside, London SE1 9TG, United Kingdom +44 207 401 5167

...And, for good measure, an entire town of bookstores:

Hay-on-Wye in Wales

"

Do not read,
as children do,
to amuse yourself,
or like the ambitious,
for the purpose
of instruction.
No, read in order to live.

"

—Gustave Flaubert

Very Clickable Book Websites

For the digitally inclined, here's a dozen delectable book sites:

Abebooks. www.abebooks.com

Alibris. www.alibris.com

Amazon. www.amazon.com

Barnes & Noble. www.barnesandnoble.com

Betterworldbooks. www.betterworldbooks.com

Bookfinder. www.bookfinder.com

Bookriot. www.bookriot.com

GoodReads. www.goodreads.com

Library Thing. www.librarything.com

The Millions. www.themillions.com

The Staff Recommends. www.thestaffrecommends.com

Tomfolio. www.tomfolio.com

Waterstones. www.waterstones.com

In addition to this batch, all of the bookstores and literary pilgrimages listed in previous sections maintain websites worthy of your attention.

Award-Winning Books and Authors

Book that are considered to be the best don't spoil or lose their luster. Early works by Alice Walker or Anne Tyler, or even Jane Austen and Virginia Woolf, somehow retain their magic decades, or even centuries, later. Thus, lists of noteworthy or award-winning books from the past aren't just empty cavalcades of brittle history, but bountiful fields waiting to be harvested.

In that spirit, gathered here are several of the most significant award groupings. Because of limited space, only selections from 1980 to the present are listed for the following:

- **THE MODERN LIBRARY 100 BEST TWENTIETH-CENTURY NOVELS AND NONFICTION**

- **THE NATIONAL BOOK AWARD FOR FICTION AND NONFICTION**

- **THE PULITZER PRIZE FOR FICTION AND NONFICTION**

- **THE MAN BOOKER PRIZE**

- **THE NOBEL PRIZE IN LITERATURE**

- **THE NEW YORK PUBLIC LIBRARY'S MOST BORROWED BOOKS**

- **OPRAH'S BOOK CLUB**

- **OPRAH'S BOOK CLUB 2.0**

THE MODERN LIBRARY'S 100 BEST NOVELS

1   *Ulysses* by James Joyce
2   *The Great Gatsby* by F. Scott Fitzgerald
3   *A Portrait of the Artist as a Young Man* by James Joyce
4   *Lolita* by Vladimir Nabokov
5   *Brave New World* by Aldous Huxley
6   *The Sound and the Fury* by William Faulkner
7   *Catch-22* by Joseph Heller
8   *Darkness at Noon* by Arthur Koestler
9   *Sons and Lovers* by D. H. Lawrence
10 *The Grapes of Wrath by John Steinbeck*
11 *Under the Volcano* by Malcolm Lowry
12 *The Way of All Flesh* by Samuel Butler
13 *1984* by George Orwell
14 *I, Claudius* by Robert Graves
15 *To the Lighthouse* by Virginia Woolf
16 *An American Tragedy* by Theodore Dreiser
17 *The Heart Is a Lonely Hunter* by Carson McCullers
18 *Slaughterhouse-Five* by Kurt Vonnegut
19 *Invisible Man* by Ralph Ellison
20 *Native Son* by Richard Wright
21 *Henderson the Rain King* by Saul Bellow
22 *Appointment in Samarra* by John O'Hara
23 *U.S.A.* (trilogy) by John Dos Passos
24 *Winesburg, Ohio* by Sherwood Anderson
25 *A Passage to India* by E. M. Forster
26 *The Wings of the Dove* by Henry James
27 *The Ambassadors* by Henry James
28 *Tender Is the Night* by F. Scott Fitzgerald
29 *The Studs Lonigan Trilogy* by James T. Farrell
30 *The Good Soldier* by Ford Madox Ford
31 *Animal Farm* by George Orwell
32 *The Golden Bowl* by Henry James
33 *Sister Carrie* by Theodore Dreiser
34 *A Handful of Dust* by Evelyn Waugh
35 *As I Lay Dying* by William Faulkner

36   *All the King's Men* by Robert Penn Warren
37   *The Bridge of San Luis Rey* by Thornton Wilder
38   *Howard's End* by E. M. Forster
39   *Go Tell It on the Mountain* by James Baldwin
40   *The Heart of the Matter* by Graham Greene
41   *Lord of the Flies* by William Golding
42   *Deliverance* by James Dickey
43   *A Dance to the Music of Time* (series) by Anthony Powell
44   *Point Counter Point* by Aldous Huxley
45   *The Sun Also Rises* by Ernest Hemingway
46   *The Secret Agent* by Joseph Conrad
47   *Nostromo* by Joseph Conrad
48   *The Rainbow* by D. H. Lawrence
49   *Women in Love* by D. H. Lawrence
50   *Tropic of Cancer* by Henry Miller
51   *The Naked and the Dead* by Norman Mailer
52   *Portnoy's Complaint* by Philip Roth
53   *Pale Fire* by Vladimir Nabokov
54   *Light in August* by William Faulkner
55   *On the Road* by Jack Kerouac
56   *The Maltese Falcon* by Dashiell Hammett
57   *Parade's End* by Ford Madox Ford
58   *The Age of Innocence* by Edith Wharton
59   *Zuleika Dobson* by Max Beerbohm
60   *The Moviegoer* by Walker Percy
61   *Death Comes for the Archbishop* by Willa Cather
62   *From Here to Eternity* by James Jones
63   *The Wapshot Chronicles* by John Cheever
64   *The Catcher in the Rye* by J. D. Salinger
65   *A Clockwork Orange* by Anthony Burgess
66   *Of Human Bondage* by W. Somerset Maugham
67   *Heart of Darkness* by Joseph Conrad
68   *Main Street* by Sinclair Lewis
69   *The House of Mirth* by Edith Wharton
70   *The Alexandria Quartet* by Lawrence Durell
71   *A High Wind in Jamaica* by Richard Hughes

72 *A House For Mr. Biswas* by V. S. Naipaul
73 *The Day of the Locust* by Nathanael West
74 *A Farewell to Arms* by Ernest Hemingway
75 *Scoop* by Evelyn Waugh
76 *The Prime of Miss Jean Brodie* by Muriel Spark
77 *Finnegans Wake* by James Joyce
78 *Kim* by Rudyard Kipling
79 *A Room with a View* by E. M. Forster
80 *Brideshead Revisited* by Evelyn Waugh
81 *The Adventures of Augie March* by Saul Bellow
82 *Angle of Repose* by Wallace Stegner
83 *A Bend in the River* by V. S. Naipaul
84 *The Death of the Heart* by Elizabeth Bowen
85 *Lord Jim* by Joseph Conrad
86 *Ragtime* by E. L. Doctorow
87 *The Old Wives' Tale* by Arnold Bennett
88 *The Call of the Wild* by Jack London
89 *Loving* by Henry Green
90 *Midnight's Children* by Salman Rushdie
91 *Tobacco Road* by Erskine Caldwell
92 *Ironweed* by William Kennedy
93 *The Magus* by John Fowles
94 *Wide Sargasso Sea* by Jean Rhys
95 *Under the Net* by Iris Murdoch
96 *Sophie's Choice* by William Styron
97 *The Sheltering Sky* by Paul Bowles
98 *The Postman Always Rings Twice* by James M. Cain
99 *The Ginger Man* by J. P. Donleavy
100 *The Magnificent Ambersons* by Booth Tarkington

THE MODERN LIBRARY'S 100 BEST NONFICTION
1 *The Education of Henry Adams* by Henry Adams
2 *The Varieties of Religious Experience* by William James
3 *Up from Slavery* by Booker T. Washington
4 *A Room of One's Own* by Virginia Woolf
5 *Silent Spring* by Rachel Carson

76 *The City in History* by Lewis Mumford
77 *Battle Cry of Freedom* by James M. McPherson
78 *Why We Can't Wait* by Martin Luther King, Jr.
79 *The Rise of Theodore Roosevelt* by Edmund Morris
80 *Studies in Iconology* by Erwin Panofsky
81 *The Face of Battle* by John Keegan
82 *The Strange Death of Liberal England* by George Dangerfield
83 *Vermeer* by Lawrence Gowing
84 *A Bright Shining Lie* by Neil Sheehan
85 *West with the Night* by Beryl Markham
86 *This Boy's Life* by Tobias Wolff
87 *A Mathematician's Apology* by G. H. Hardy
88 *Six Easy Pieces* by Richard P. Feynman
89 *Pilgrim at Tinker Creek* by Annie Dillard
90 *The Golden Bough* by James George Frazer
91 *Shadow and Act* by Ralph Ellison
92 *The Power Broker* by Robert A. Caro
93 *The American Political Tradition* by Richard Hofstadter
94 *The Contours of American History* by
    William Appleman Williams
95 *The Promise of American Life* by Herbert Croly
96 *In Cold Blood* by Truman Capote
97 *The Journalist and the Murderer* by Janet Malcolm
98 *The Taming of Chance* by Ian Hacking
99 *Operating Instructions* by Anne Lamott
100 *Melbourne* by Lord David Cecil

THE NATIONAL BOOK AWARD FOR FICTION

1980 *Sophie's Choice* by William Styron
1981 *Plains Song* by Wright Morris
1982 *Rabbit Is Rich* by John Updike
1983 *The Color Purple* by Alice Walker
1984 *Victory Over Japan: A Book of Stories* by Ellen Gilchrist
1985 *White Noise* by Don DeLillo
1986 *World's Fair* by E. L. Doctorow
1987 *Paco's Story* by Larry Heinemann

1988 *Paris Trout* by Pete Dexter
1989 *Spartina* by John Casey
1990 *Middle Passage* by Charles Johnson
1991 *Mating* by Norman Rush
1992 *All the Pretty Horses* by Cormac McCarthy
1993 *The Shipping News* by E. Annie Proulx
1994 *A Frolic of His Own* by William Gaddis
1995 *Sabbath's Theater* by Philip Roth
1996 *Ship Fever and Other Stories* by Andrea Barrett
1997 *Cold Mountain* by Charles Frazier
1998 *Charming Billy* by Alice McDermott
1999 *Waiting* by Ha Jin
2000 *In America* by Susan Sontag
2001 *The Corrections* by Jonathan Franzen
2002 *Three Junes* by Julia Glass
2003 *The Great Fire* by Shirley Hazzard
2004 *The News from Paraguay* by Lily Tuck
2005 *Europe Central* by William T. Vollmann
2006 *The Echo Maker* by Richard Powers
2007 *Tree of Smoke* by Denis Johnson
2008 *Shadow Country* by Peter Matthiessen
2009 *Let the Great World Spin* by Colum McCann
2010 *Lord of Misrule* by Jaimy Gordon
2011 *Salvage the Bones* by Jesmyn Ward
2012 *The Round House* by Louise Erdrich
2013 *The Good Lord Bird* by James McBride
2014 *Redeployment by Phil Klay*
2015 *Fortune Smiles: Stories by Adam Johnson*

THE NATIONAL BOOK AWARD FOR HISTORY

1980 *The White House Years* by Henry A. Kissinger
1981 *Christianity, Social Tolerance, and Homosexuality* by John
      Boswell
1982 *People of the Sacred Mountain: A History of the Northern*
      Cheyenne Chiefs and Warrior Societies, 1830–1879
      by Father Peter John Powell

1983 *Voices of Protest: Huey Long, Father Coughlin, and the Great Depression* by Alan Brinkley

THE NATIONAL BOOK AWARD FOR SCIENCE

1980 *Gödel, Escher, Bach: An Eternal Golden Braid* by Douglas Hofstadter

1981 *The Panda's Thumb: More Reflections on Natural History* by Stephen Jay Gould

1982 *Lucy: The Beginnings of Humankind* by Donald C. Johanson & Maitland A. Edey

1983 *Subtle Is the Lord: The Science and Life of Albert Einstein* by Abraham Pais

THE NATIONAL BOOK AWARD FOR NONFICTION

1984 *Andrew Jackson and the Course of American Democracy, 1833–1845* by Robert V. Remini

1985 *Common Ground: A Turbulent Decade in the Lives of Three American Families* by J. Anthony Lukas

1986 *Arctic Dreams* by Barry Lopez

1987 *The Making of the Atom Bomb* by Richard Rhodes

1988 *A Bright Shining Lie: John Paul Vann and America in Vietnam* by Neil Sheehan

1989 *From Beirut to Jerusalem* by Thomas L. Friedman

1990 *The House of Morgan: An American Banking Dynasty and the Rise of Modern Finance* by Ron Chernow

1991 *Freedom* by Orlando Patterson

1992 *Becoming a Man: Half a Life Story* by Paul Monette

1993 *United States: Essays 1952–1992* by Gore Vidal

1994 *How We Die: Reflections on Life's Final Chapter* by Sherwin B. Nuland

1995 *The Haunted Land: Facing Europe's Ghosts After Communism* by Tina Rosenberg

1996 *An American Requiem: God, My Father, and the War That Came Between Us* by James Carroll

1997 *American Sphinx: The Character of Thomas Jefferson* by Joseph J. Ellis

1998 *Slaves in the Family* by Edward Ball

1999 *Embracing Defeat: Japan in the Wake of World War II*
by John W. Dower

2000 *In the Heart of the Sea: The Tragedy of the Whaleship Essex* by Nathaniel Philbrick

2001 *The Noonday Demon: An Atlas of Depression*
by Andrew Solomon

2002 *Master of the Senate: The Years of Lyndon Johnson*
by Robert A. Caro

2003 *Waiting for Snow in Havana: Confessions of a Cuban Boy*
by Carlos Eire

2004 *Arc of Justice: A Saga of Race, Civil Rights, and Murder in the Jazz Age* by Kevin Boyle

2005 *The Year of Magical Thinking* by Joan Didion

2006 *The Worst Hard Time: The Untold Story of Those Who Survived the Great American Dust Bowl* by Timothy Egan

2007 *Legacy of Ashes: The History of the CIA* by Tim Weiner

2008 *The Hemingses of Monticello: An American Family*
by Annette Gordon-Reed

2009 *The First Tycoon: The Epic Life of Cornelius Vanderbilt*
by T. J. Stiles

2010 *Just Kids* by Patti Smith

2011 *The Swerve: How the World Became Modern*
by Stephen Greenblatt

2012 *Behind the Beautiful Forevers: Life, Death, and Hope in a Mumbai Undercity* by Katherine Boo

2013 *The Unwinding: An Inner History of the New America*
by George Packer

2014 *Age of Ambition: Chasing Fortune, Truth, and Faith in the New China* by Evan Osnos

2015 *Between the World and Me* by Ta-Nehisi Coates

THE PULITZER PRIZE FOR FICTION

1980 *The Executioner's Song* by Norman Mailer

1981 *A Confederacy of Dunces* by John Kennedy Toole

1982 *Rabbit Is Rich* by John Updike

1983 *The Color Purple* by Alice Walker

1984 *Ironweed* by William Kennedy
1985 *Foreign Affairs* by Alison Lurie
1986 *Lonesome Dove* by Larry McMurtry
1987 *A Summons to Memphis* by Peter Taylor
1988 *Beloved* by Toni Morrison
1989 *Breathing Lessons* by Anne Tyler
1990 *The Mambo Kings Play Songs of Love* by Oscar Hijuelos
1991 *Rabbit at Rest* by John Updike
1992 *A Thousand Acres* by Jane Smiley
1993 *A Good Scent from a Strange Mountain*
       by Robert Olen Butler
1994 *The Shipping News* by E. Annie Proulx
1995 *The Stone Diaries* by Carol Shields
1996 *Independence Day* by Richard Ford
1997 *Martin Dressler: The Tale of an American Dreamer*
       by Steven Millhauser
1998 *American Pastoral* by Philip Roth
1999 *The Hours* by Michael Cunningham
2000 *Interpreter of Maladies* by Jhumpa Lahiri
2001 *The Amazing Adventures of Kavalier & Clay*
       by Michael Chabon
2002 *Empire Falls* by Richard Russo
2003 *Middlesex* by Jeffrey Eugenides
2004 *The Known World* by Edward P. Jones
2005 *Gilead* by Marilynne Robinson
2006 *March* by Geraldine Brooks
2007 *The Road* by Cormac McCarthy
2008 *The Brief Wondrous Life of Oscar Wao* by Junot Díaz
2009 *Olive Kitteridge* by Elizabeth Strout
2010 *Tinkers* by Paul Harding
2011 *A Visit From the Goon Squad* by Jennifer Egan
2012 No award given.
2013 *The Orphan Master's Son* by Adam Johnson
2014 *The Goldfinch* by Donna Tartt
2015 *All the Light We Cannot See by Anthony Doerr*
2016 *The Sympathizer* by Viet Thanh Nguyen

THE PULITZER PRIZE FOR GENERAL NONFICTION

1980 *Gödel, Escher, Bach: An Eternal Golden Braid*
      by Douglas Hofstadter

1981 *Fin-de-Siècle Vienna: Politics and Culture*
      by Carl E. Schorske

1982 *The Soul of a New Machine* by Tracy Kidder

1983 *Is There No Place on Earth for Me?* by Susan Sheehan

1984 *The Social Transformation of American Medicine* by Paul Starr

1985 *The Good War: An Oral History of World War Two* by Studs Terkel

1986 (two winners) *Common Ground: A Turbulent Decade in the
      Lives of Three American Families* by J. Anthony Lukas
      and *Move Your Shadow: South Africa, Black and
      White* by Joseph Lelyveld

1987 *Arab and Jew: Wounded Spirits in a Promised Land*
      by David K. Shipler

1988 *The Making of the Atomic Bomb* by Richard Rhodes

1989 *A Bright Shining Lie: John Paul Vann and America in
      Vietnam* by Neil Sheehan

1990 *And Their Children After Them* by Dale Maharidge
      and Michael Williamson

1991 *The Ants* by Bert Hölldobler and Edward O. Wilson

1992 *The Prize: The Epic Quest for Oil, Money, andPower*
      by Daniel Yergin

1993 *Lincoln at Gettysburg: The Words That Remade America*
      by Garry Wills

1994 *Lenin's Tomb: The Last Days of the Soviet Empire*
      by David Remnick

1995 *The Beak of the Finch: A Story of Evolution in Our Time*
      by Jonathan Weiner

1996 *The Haunted Land: Facing Europe's Ghosts After
      Communism* by Tina Rosenberg

1997 *Ashes to Ashes: America's Hundred-Year Cigarette War,
      the Public Health, and the Unabashed Triumph of Philip
      Morris* by Richard Kluger

1998 *Guns, Germs, and Steel: The Fates of Human Societies*
      by Jared Diamond

THE PULITZER PRIZE FOR HISTORY

1980 *Been in the Storm So Long* by Leon F. Litwack

1981 *American Education: The National Experience,
1783–1876* by Lawrence A. Cremin

1982 *Mary Chesnut's Civil War* by C. Vann Woodward

1983 *The Transformation of Virginia, 1740–1790* by Rhys L. Isaac

1984 No award given.

1985 *Prophets of Regulation* by Thomas K. McCraw

1986 *...the Heavens and the Earth: A Political History of the
Space Age* by Walter A. McDougall

1987 *Voyagers to the West: A Passage in the Peopling of America
on the Eve of the Revolution* by Bernard Bailyn

1988 *The Launching of Modern American Science,
1846–1876* by Robert V. Bruce

1989 (two winners) *Battle Cry of Freedom: The Civil War Era*
by James M. McPherson and *Parting the Waters:
America in theKing Years 1954–1963* by Taylor Branch

1990 *In Our Image: America's Empire in the Philippines*
by Stanley Karnow

1991 *A Midwife's Tale* by Laurel Thatcher Ulrich

1992 *The Fate of Liberty: Abraham Lincoln and Civil
Liberties* by Mark E. Neely Jr.

1993 *The Radicalism of the American Revolution* by Gordon S. Wood

1994 No award given.

1995 *No Ordinary Time: Franklin and Eleanor Roosevelt:
The Home Front in World War II* by Doris Kearns Goodwin

1996 *William Cooper's Town: Power and Persuasion on the
Frontier of the Early American Republic* by Alan Taylor

1997 *Original Meanings: Politics and Ideas in the Making of the
Constitution* by Jack N. Rakove

1998 *Summer for the Gods: The Scopes Trial and America's
Continuing Debate Over Science and Religion*
by Edward J. Larson

1999 *Gotham: A History of New York City to 1898*
by Edwin G. Burrows and Mike Wallace

2000 *Freedom from Fear: The American People in Depression*

and War, 1929–1945 by David M. Kennedy

THE PULITZER PRIZE FOR BIOGRAPHY OR AUTOBIOGRAPHY

2010	*The First Tycoon: The Epic Life of Cornelius Vanderbilt* by T. J. Stiles
2011	*Washington: A Life* by Ron Chernow
2012	*George F. Kennan: An American Life* by John Lewis Gaddis
2013	*The Black Count: Glory, Revolution, Betrayal, and the Real Count of Monte Cristo* by Tom Reiss
2014	*Margaret Fuller: A New American Life* by Megan Marshall
2015	*The Pope and Mussolini: The Secret History of Pius XI and the Rise of Fascism in Europe* by David I. Kertzer
2016	*Barbarian Days: A Surfing Life* by William Finnegan

THE PULITZER PRIZE FOR POETRY

1980	*Selected Poems* by Donald Justice
1981	*The Morning of the Poem* by James Schuyler
1982	*The Collected Poems* by Sylvia Plath
1983	*Selected Poems* by Galway Kinnell
1984	*American Primitive* by Mary Oliver
1985	*Yin* by Carolyn Kizer
1986	*The Flying Change* by Henry S. Taylor
1987	*Thomas and Beulah* by Rita Dove
1988	*Partial Accounts: New and Selected Poems* by William Meredith
1989	*New and Collected Poems* by Richard Wilbur
1990	*The World Doesn't End* by Charles Simic
1991	*Near Changes* by Mona Van Duyn
1992	*Selected Poems* by James Tate
1993	*The Wild Iris* by Louise Glück
1994	*Neon Vernacular: New and Selected Poems* by Yusef Komunyakaa
1995	*The Simple Truth* by Philip Levine
1996	*The Dream of the Unified Field* by Jorie Graham
1997	*Alive Together: New and Selected Poems* by Lisel Mueller
1998	*Black Zodiac* by Charles Wright
1999	*Blizzard of One* by Mark Strand
2000	*Repair* by C. K. Williams
2001	*Different Hours* by Stephen Dunn

2002	*Practical Gods* by Carl Dennis
2003	*Moy Sand and Gravel* by Paul Muldoon
2004	*Walking to Martha's Vineyard* by Franz Wright
2005	*Delights & Shadows* by Ted Kooser
2006	*Late Wife* by Claudia Emerson
2007	*Native Guard* by Natasha Trethewey
2008	(two winners) *Time and Materials* by Robert Hass and *Failure* by Philip Schultz
2009	*The Shadow of Sirius* by W. S. Merwin
2010	*Versed* by Rae Armantrout
2011	*The Best of It: New and Selected Poems* by Kay Ryan
2012	*Life on Mars* by Tracy K. Smith
2013	*Stag's Leap* by Sharon Olds
2014	*3 Sections* by Vijay Seshadri
2015	*Digest* by Gregory Pardlo
2016	*Ozone Journal* by Peter Balakian

THE MAN BOOKER PRIZE

1980	*The Beggar Maid* by Alice Munroe
1981	*Midnight's Children* by Salman Rushdie
1982	*Schindler's Ark* by Thomas Keneally
1983	*Life & Times of Michael K* by J. M. Coetzee
1984	*Hotel du Luc* by Anita Brookner
1985	*The Bone People* by Keri Hulme
1986	*The Old Devil* by Kingsley Amis
1987	*Moon Tiger* by Penelope Lively
1988	*Oscar and Lucinda* by Peter Carey
1989	*The Remains of the Day* by Kazuo Ishiguro
1990	*Possession: A Romance* by A. S. Byatt
1991	*The Famished Road* by Ben Okra
1992	*The English Patient* by Michael Ondaatje
1993	*Paddy Clarke Ha Ha Ha* by Roddy Doyle
1994	*How Late It Was, How Late* by James Kelman
1995	*The Ghost Road* by Pat Barker
1996	*Last Orders* by Graham Swift
1997	*The God of Small Things* by Arundhati Roy

1998   *Amsterdam* by Ian McEwan
1999   *Disgrace* by J. M. Coetzee
2000   *The Blind Assassin* by Margaret Atwood
2001   *True History of the Kelly Gang* by Peter Carey
2002   *Life of Pi* by Yann Martel
2003   *Vernon God Little* by DBC Pierre
2004   *The Line of Beauty* by Alan Hollinghurst
2005   *The Sea* by Jon Banville
2006   *The Inheritance of Loss* by Kiran Desai
2007   *The Gathering* by Ann Enright
2008   *The White Tiger* by Aravind Adiga
2009   *Wolf Hall* by Hilary Mantel
2010   *The Finkler Question* by Howard Jacobson
2011   *The Sense of an Ending* by Julian Barnes
2012   *Bring Up the Bodies* by Hilary Mantel
2013   *The Luminaries* by Eleanor Catton
2014   *The Narrow Road to the Deep North* by Richard Flanagan
2015   *A Brief History of Seven Killings* by Marlon James

THE NOBEL PRIZE IN LITERATURE
1980   Czeslaw Milosz, Poland and the United States
1981   Elias Canetti, United Kingdom
1982   Gabriel García Márquez, Colombia
1983   William Golding, United Kingdom
1984   Jaroslav Seifert, Czechoslovakia
1985   Claude Simon, France
1986   Wole Soyinka, Nigeria
1987   Joseph Brodsky, United States
1988   Naguib Mahfouz, Egypt
1989   Camilo José Cela, Spain
1990   Octavio Paz, Mexico
1991   Nadine Gordimer, South Africa
1992   Derek Walcott, Saint Lucia
1993   Toni Morrison, United States
1994   Kenzaburo Oe, Japan
1995   Seamus Heaney, Ireland

1996	Wislawa Szymborska, Poland
1997	Dario Fo, Italy
1998	José Saramago, Portugal
1999	Günter Grass, Germany
2000	Gao Xingjian, France
2001	V. S. Naipaul, United Kingdom
2002	Imre Kertész, Hungary
2003	J. M. Coetzee, South Africa
2004	Elfriede Jelinek, Austria
2005	Harold Pinter, United Kingdom
2006	Orhan Pamuk, Turkey
2007	Doris Lessing, United Kingdom
2008	Jean-Marie Gustave Le Clézio, France and Mauritius
2009	Herta Müller, Romania and Germany
2010	Mario Vargas Llosa, Peru
2011	Tomas Tranströmer, Sweden
2012	Mo Yan, China
2013	Alice Munro, Canada
2014	Patrick Modiano, France
2015	Svetlana Alexievich, Belarus

THE NEW YORK PUBLIC LIBRARY'S MOST BORROWED BOOKS IN 2015

1. *Leaving Time* by Jodi Picoult
2. *The Paying Guests* by Sarah Waters
3. *In the Unlikely Event* by Judy Blume
4. *Not That Kind of Girl* by Lena Dunham
5. *Gone Girl* by Gillian Flynn
6. *Prodigal Son* by Danielle Steel
7. *NYPD Red 3* by Marshall Karp and James Patterson
8. *Go Set a Watchman* by Harper Lee
9. *The Girl on the Train* by Paula Hawkins
10. *Grey* by E. L. James

OPRAH'S BOOK CLUB
1996
The Deep End of the Ocean by Jacquelyn Mitchard
Song of Solomon by Toni Morrison
The Book of Ruth by Jane Hamilton
She's Come Undone by Wally Lamb

1997
Stones from the River by Ursula Hegi
The Rapture of Canaan by Sheri Reynolds
The Heart of a Woman by Maya Angelou
Songs in Ordinary Time by Mary McGarry Morris
The Meanest Thing to Say by Bill Cosby
A Lesson Before Dying by Ernest J. Gaines
A Virtuous Woman by Kaye Gibbons
Ellen Foster by Kaye Gibbons
The Treasure Hunt by Bill Cosby
The Best Way to Play by Bill Cosby

1998

Paradise by Toni Morrison
Here on Earth by Alice Hoffman
Black and Blue by Anna Quindlen
Breath, Eyes, Memory by Edwidge Danticat
I Know This Much Is True by Wally Lamb
What Looks Like Crazy on an Ordinary Day by Pearl Cleage
Midwives by Chris Bohjalian
Where the Heart Is by Billie Letts

1999

Jewel by Bret Lott
The Reader by Bernhard Schlink
The Pilot's Wife by Anita Shreve
White Oleander by Janet Fitch
Mother of Pearl by Melinda Haynes
Tara Road by Maeve Binchy
River, Cross My Heart by Breena Clarke
Vinegar Hill by A. Manette Ansay
A Map of the World by Jane Hamilton

2000

Gap Creek by Robert Morgan
Daughter of Fortune by Isabel Allende
Back Roads by Tawni O'Dell
The Bluest Eye by Toni Morrison
While I Was Gone by Sue Miller
The Poisonwood Bible by Barbara Kingsolver
Open House by Elizabeth Berg
Drowning Ruth by Christina Schwarz
House of Sand and Fog by Andre Dubus III

2001

We Were the Mulvaneys by Joyce Carol Oates
Icy Sparks by Gwyn Hyman Rubio
Stolen Lives: Twenty Years in a Desert Jail by Malika Oufkir

Cane River by Lalita Tademy
The Corrections by Jonathan Franzen
A Fine Balance by Rohinton Mistry

2002

Fall on Your Knees by Ann-Marie MacDonald
Sula by Toni Morrison

2003

East of Eden by John Steinbeck
Cry, the Beloved Country by Alan Paton

2004

One Hundred Years of Solitude by Gabriel García Márquez
The Heart Is a Lonely Hunter by Carson McCullers
Anna Karenina by Leo Tolstoy
The Good Earth by Pearl S. Buck

2005

The Sound and the Fury; As I Lay Dying; Light in August
    by William Faulkner
A Million Little Pieces by James Frey

2006

Night by Elie Wiesel

2007

The Measure of a Man: A Spiritual Autobiography by Sir Sidney Poitier
The Road by Cormac McCarthy
Middlesex by Jeffrey Eugenides
Love in the Time of Cholera by Gabriel García Márquez
The Pillars of the Earth by Ken Follett

2008

A New Earth by Eckhart Tolle
The Story of Edgar Sawtelle by David Wroblewski

2009
Say You're One of Them by Uwem Akpan

2010
Freedom by Jonathan Franzen
Great Expectations; A Tale of Two Cities by Charles Dickens

OPRAH'S BOOK CLUB 2.0
2012
Wild: From Lost to Found on the Pacific Crest Trail by Cheryl Strayed
The Twelve Tribes of Hattie by Ayan Matthis

2014
The Invention of Wings by Sue Monk Kid

2015
Ruby by Cynthia Bond

2016
The Underground Railroad by Colson Whitehead
Love Warrior by Glennon Doyle Melton

A Note by the Compiler

If I were a determined determinist, I would imagine that I was destined to preside over a journal about reading. During my childhood, polio, bronchitis, scarlet fever, and other maladies made me an invalid incapable of being the centerfielder I wanted to be. I responded by turning my sickroom into a library. Besides perusing my latest finds, my greatest joys were my foraging adventures with my father to the Fourth Avenue shops of Manhattan's "used bookstore row" and our rhapsodic afternoons at the New York Public Library. My first job, quite logically, was in the Westfield Public Library. In college, I renewed my obsession, skipping meals to buy books. Since then, I have spent decades working in two bookstores, helping customers, running a book information service, and purchasing private libraries; writing and editing magazines about books; and writing, editing, and publishing books myself. I cannot imagine a day without reading and, yet with all these words, I have never been able to adequately express the pleasures it has given me.